can Americans

ALI

Champion Boxer

Norman D.
Graubart

E Enslow Publishing
101 W. 23rd Street
Suite 240
New York, NY 10011
USA

enslow.com

Words to Know

championship—A title that means a person is the best at a sport or competition.

knockout— A punch that makes the other boxer unable to recover.

match—A sporting competition.

Muslim—A person who follows the religion of Islam.

nerves—Thin bands in the body that control movement and send messages to and from the brain.

Parkinson's disease—A sickness that affects the nerves and makes it hard to control movements.

philanthropist—A person who donates money or effort to an important cause.

technical knockout—The end of a boxing match when the referee decides that it is unsafe for a fighter to continue, usually because of injuries.

Contents

Laila Ali

CHAPTER 1

The Family Business

Laila Ali was born on December 30, 1977, in Miami Beach, Florida. Her mother is an actress named Veronica Porsche Ali. Her father is a very famous boxer named Muhammad Ali. Muhammad Ali was born with the name Cassius Clay, but he changed his name when he became a **Muslim**.

Many people who love boxing think that Muhammad Ali is the greatest boxer of all time. He changed the way that boxers moved and punched. One of his tricks was to make the other boxer throw a lot of punches so he would get tired.

He has not fought a **match** in over thirty years, but he is still thought to be one of the best boxers ever.

When Laila was young, some kids would pick fights with her. She says they did this because they wanted to see if Muhammad Ali's daughter was a good fighter. Laila decided to become a boxer when

Laila Says:

"Obviously I grew up with my dad being Muhammad Ali, around a lot of attention, and [boxing] was...something that I tried to run away from."

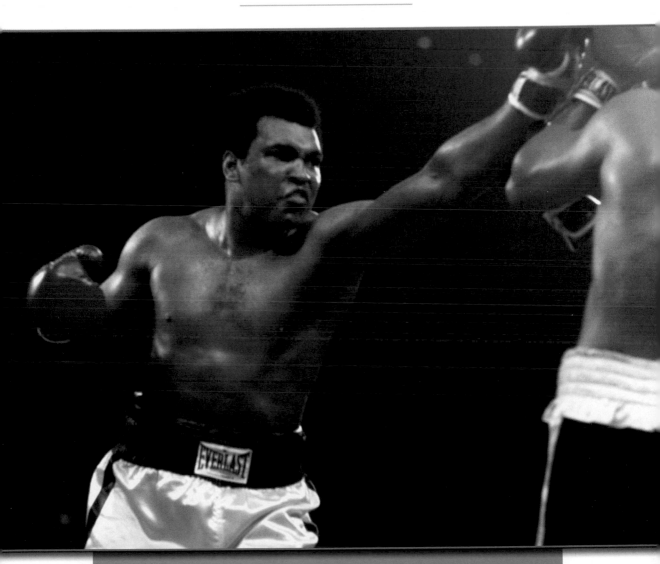

Laila's father, Muhammad Ali, hits an opponent. Ali's nickname is "The Greatest."

she was eighteen. She was getting ready to watch a boxing match with famous boxer Mike Tyson. Then she noticed that there were two women who fought right before Tyson's fight. Laila says from the moment she saw those women boxing, she wanted to do it too.

CHAPTER 2

Becoming a Boxing Star

When Laila told her dad that she wanted to be a boxer, Muhammad Ali was not very happy. After many fights, her father had gotten an illness called **Parkinson's disease**. Parkinson's disease affects the **nerves** and can cause the arms and legs to shake. While doctors don't know for sure if Ali got the disease from being hit in the head so many times, it's very likely that that's what happened. So, he was worried when Laila said she wanted to be a boxer. But she promised to be safe and to train well.

Laila poses with her dad after she won a fight against Erin Toughill and kept her middleweight title.

Laila's first fight was against April Fowler in 1999. Laila won the fight with a **knockout** in the first round. Laila kept on winning matches. She fought at least two fights a year for the next few years, and won all of them.

Laila Says:

"Because I come from a successful family, [people] think success came naturally. It didn't. I have had to work hard for whatever I've accomplished."

Laila throws a punch at Shelley Burton, who challenged her for the middleweight title. Laila won this fight.

Boxers fight against other people who are in the same weight class. Laila was a middleweight for most of her career. She first fought for the middleweight **championship** title in August 2002 against Suzette Taylor and she won. Up to this point, Laila had still not lost a fight. She was beginning to look a lot like her dad.

Laila spent many hours practicing in boxing rings like this one.

CHAPTER 3

A Historic Match

When Muhammad Ali was boxing, the other most famous boxer was Joe Frazier. Frazier was a heavyweight, just like Muhammad Ali, and they were both very good. They were both undefeated in 1971 when they fought for the heavyweight title. This fight was called the Fight of the Century, and Frazier won. Ali challenged Frazier two more times and won both times. Boxing fans still argue about who was a better boxer.

When Joe Frazier's daughter, Jacqui Frazier-Lyde, saw Laila boxing, she was inspired to start training too.

Muhammad Ali fights Joe Frazier in the Fight of the Century. Years later, their daughters fought each other.

After some training and practice fights, Frazier-Lyde challenged Laila to a match. Newspapers and the media called the match Ali-Frazier IV, because their fathers had fought three times before.

Many boxing matches end before all of the rounds have been fought. This is because one of the boxers gets so tired or beaten up that the judges stop the fight. This is called a **technical knockout**. But this

Laila Says:

> "I've trained harder, I'm better, I'm stronger, the blood of a champion runs through my veins...I've already won."

fight went all eight rounds. One judge thought that Laila and Frazier-Lyde tied. But the other two judges thought Laila fought better, which means that she won the fight. While Frazier-Lyde was a good challenger, Laila kept the victory in her family.

Laila (left) and Jacqui Frazier-Lyde pose with their fists out to promote their fight.

CHAPTER 4

After Boxing

Laila stopped boxing in 2007. In her last fight, she kept the middleweight championship title, so she retired as a champion boxer. Laila has done many different things since she left boxing. She became a fitness trainer and made some fitness training videos in 2007. Her partner in the videos is Sugar Ray Leonard, who is another one of the best boxers of all time.

Today, Laila is a host on two television shows. One of the shows is called *Late Night Chef Fight*, which has cooking competitions. Laila loves to cook and she loves to fight, so this is a perfect show for her to host! Laila's other show is called *All In With*

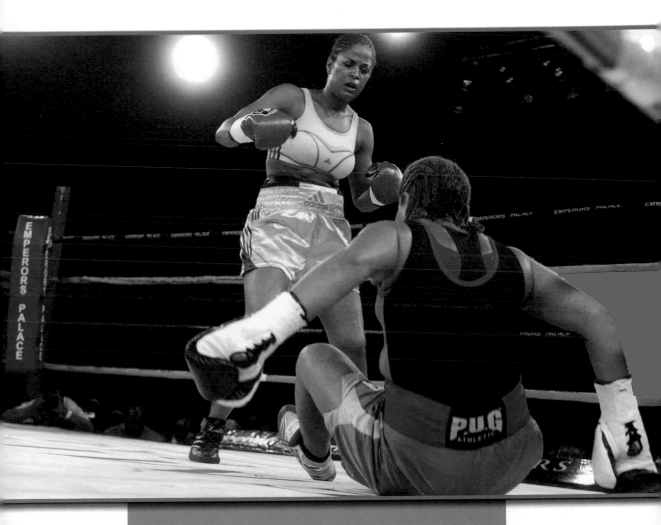

Laila knocks down Gwendolyn O'Neill during Laila's last professional fight.

Laila Ali. She goes around the world to find stories about amazing people.

But Laila has done more with her fame than just work on TV shows. She is also a **philanthropist**. Philanthropists are people who find ways to give money and other kinds of help to people in need. Because of her interest in fitness, health, and sports, she donates her time and money to Feeding America and the Women's Sports Foundation.

WOMEN'S SPORTS FOUNDATION

Laila speaks to members of the Women's Sports Foundation. This is one of the ways she gives back to the community.

Laila Ali is someone who was born with fame and wealth. But through her hard work and talent, she became powerful all by herself. As a champion boxer, she has shown girls that they can succeed in any sport they choose. Now, she takes the success that she has earned and spends her time giving back to others.

Laila Says:

"I never intended to box forever, and always planned to move on to do other things. So, I'm pretty much where I thought I'd be right now, undefeated and a world champion."

Timeline

1977—Laila Ali is born on December 30 in Miami Beach, Florida.

1996—Female boxing stars Christy Martin and Deirdre Gogarty have a match on national TV and Laila decides she wants to be a boxer.

1999—Laila fights her first match against April Fowler on December 8, knocking her out in the first round.

2001—Laila defeats Jacqui Frazier-Lyde in a historic matchup on June 8.

2002—Laila wins her first title match against Suzette Taylor.

2003—Laila fights Christy Martin, the woman whose boxing career inspired her to fight herself. Laila wins by a knockout.

2007—Laila fights her last professional fight on February 3. She retires undefeated and holding the middleweight championship.

2010—Laila becomes president of the Women's Sports Foundation. She serves until 2012.

2012—Laila participates in *Stars Earn Stripes*, a show that raises money for veterans.

2013—Laila begins hosting the television series *All In With Laila Ali*.

Learn More

Books

Denenberg, Barry. *Ali: An American Champion.* New York: Simon & Schuster, 2014.

Sutherland, Adam. *Athletes (Black History Makers).* New York: Rosen, 2012.

Ungs, Tim. *Famous Families: Muhammad Ali and Laila Ali.* New York: Rosen, 2005.

Web Sites

womenboxing.com/lailaali.htm
Includes photos and a detailed account of Laila's boxing career.

mrnussbaum.com/athletes/muhammed_ali/
Provides a brief biography as well as video of Muhammad Ali.

womenssportsfoundation.org/
Learn more about the Women's Sports Foundation, which supports women and girls in sports and physical activity.

Index

Published in 2016 by Enslow Publishing, LLC.
101 W. 23rd Street, Suite 240, New York, NY 10011

Copyright © 2016 by Enslow Publishing, LLC.

All rights reserved.

No part of this book may be reproduced by any means without the written permission of the publisher.

Library of Congress Cataloging-in-Publication Data
Graubart, Norman D.
  Laila Ali: Champion Boxer / Norman D. Graubart.
    pages cm. — (Exceptional African Americans)
  Includes bibliographical references and index.
  Summary: "A biography of boxer Laila Ali"—Provided by publisher.
  ISBN 978-0-7660-6656-4 (library binding)
  ISBN 978-0-7660-7130-8 (pbk.)
  ISBN 978-0-7660-6655-7 (6-pack)
  1. Ali, Laila—Juvenile literature. 2. Boxers (Sports)—United States—Biography—Juvenile literature. 3. Women boxers—United States—Biography—Juvenile literature. I. Title.
  GV1132.A39G73 2015
  796.83092—dc23
  [B]
                    2015007451

Printed in the United States of America

To Our Readers: We have done our best to make sure all Web site addresses in this book were active and appropriate when we went to press. However, the author and the publisher have no control over and assume no liability for the material available on those Web sites or on any Web sites they may link to. Any comments or suggestions can be sent by e-mail to customerservice@enslow.com.

Photo Credits: Getty Images: Evan Agostini/Hulton Archive, p. 1; Focus On Sport, p. 7; Ed Mulholland/WireImage, p. 10; Don Emmert/AFP, p. 12; Cultura RM/Rimagine Group Limited, p. 13; Keystone/Hulton Archive, p. 15; New York Daily News Archive, p. 17; Stringer/AFP, p. 19; Bryan Bedder/Getty Images North America, p. 20; Shutterstock.com: ©Toria (blue background throughout book); Jaguar PS, p. 4; Flnur, p. 8.

Cover Credits: Evan Agostini/Hulton Archive/Getty Images (portrait of Laila Ali); ©Toria/Shutterstock.com (blue background).

9